The
Christian **Giving**
and

Rejoicing
In His
Abundance,
Sharing His
Resources

STEP 8

Bill Bright

NewLife
PUBLICATIONS
A MINISTRY OF CAMPUS CRUSADE FOR CHRIST

Ten Basic Steps Toward Christian Maturity
Step 8: The Christian and Giving

Published by
New*Life* Publications
100 Lake Hart Drive
Orlando, FL 32832-0100

Printed in the United States of America.

ISBN: 1–56399–037–7

Thomas Nelson Inc., Nashville, Tennessee, is the exclusive distributor of this book to the trade markets in the United States and the District of Columbia.

Distributed in Canada by Campus Crusade for Christ of Canada, Surrey, B.C.

Unless otherwise indicated, all Scripture references are from the *New International Version*, © 1973, 1978, 1984 by the International Bible Society. Published by Zondervan Bible Publishers, Grand Rapids, Michigan.

Scripture quotations designated TLB are from *The Living Bible*, © 1971 by Tyndale House Publishers, Wheaton, Illinois.

Scripture quotations designated NKJ are from the *New King James* version, © 1979, 1980, 1982 by Thomas Nelson Inc., Publishers, Nashville, Tennessee.

Scripture quotations designated NASB are from the *New American Standard Bible*, © 1960, 1962, 1963, 1968, 1971, 1972, 1975, 1977 by the Lockman Foundation, La Habra, California.

Any royalties from this book or the many other books by Bill Bright are dedicated to the glory of God and designated to the various ministries of Campus Crusade for Christ/*NewLife2000*.

For more information, write:

L.I.F.E.—P. O. Box 40, Flemmington Markets, 2129, Australia
Campus Crusade for Christ of Canada—Box 300, Vancouver, B.C., V6C 2X3, Canada
Campus Crusade for Christ—Fairgate House, King's Road, Tyseley, Birmingham, B11 2AA, England
Lay Institute for Evangelism—P. O. Box 8786, Auckland 3, New Zealand
Campus Crusade for Christ—Alexandra, P. O. Box 0205, Singapore 9115, Singapore
Great Commission Movement of Nigeria—P. O. Box 500, Jos, Plateau State Nigeria, West Africa
Campus Crusade for Christ International—100 Sunport Lane, Orlando, FL 32809, USA

Contents

Acknowledgments

The *Ten Basic Steps Toward Christian Maturity* series was a product of necessity. As the ministry of Campus Crusade for Christ expanded rapidly to scores of campuses across America, thousands of students committed their lives to Christ—several hundred on a single campus. Individual follow-up of all new converts soon became impossible. Who was to help them grow in their new-found faith?

A Bible study series designed for new Christians was desperately needed—a study that would stimulate individuals and groups to explore the depths and the riches of God's Word. Although several excellent studies were available, we felt the particular need of new material for these college students.

In 1955, I asked several of my fellow staff associates to assist me in the preparation of Bible studies that would stimulate both evangelism and Christian growth in a new believer. The contribution by campus staff members was especially significant because of their constant contact with students in introducing them to Christ and meeting regularly with them to disciple them. Thus, the *Ten Basic Steps Toward Christian Maturity* was the fruit of our combined labor.

Since that modest beginning, many other members of the staff have contributed generously. On occasion, for example, I found myself involved in research and writing sessions with several of our staff, all seminary graduates, some with advanced degrees and one with his doctorate in theology. More important, all were actively engaged in "winning, building, and sending men" for Christ.

For this latest edition, I want to thank Don Tanner for his professional assistance in revising, expanding, and editing the contents. I also want to thank Joette Whims and Jean Bryant for their extensive help and for joining Don and me in the editorial process.

A Personal Word

Marilyn, a missionary, had just returned to the United States for her scheduled home leave when she learned that one of her neighbor's sons had been seriously injured. The family had no insurance and was suffering financially as well as physically.

Marilyn prayed, "Lord, what would You have me do?" She sensed a nudge from the Lord to give her neighbors some money. Checking her bank account, she realized that her bank balance was a mere $200.

"Lord, how about $25?" she prayed. With $175 left over, she thought she could survive the rest of the month. However, she felt the Lord say, "No, I want you to give $100."

As she continued to question the Lord, Marilyn had no peace about anything less than $100. Finally, she wrote out a check, breathing a prayer. "Now I've done what You said, so You'll have to take care of my needs."

With a sense of joy and expectancy, Marilyn took the check across the street. Her act of sharing greatly encouraged the family, and God miraculously provided for her needs.

Two days later a check for $100 arrived in the mail. Three days later a woman dropped off a check for $200—something she had wanted to do for some time, she told Marilyn.

Within five days of writing her check, Marilyn received from unexpected sources a total of $500.

Marilyn discovered one of the greatest privileges and blessings of the Christian life: the wonderful adventure of giving by faith.

The average Christian is unaware of the basic principles of giving by faith that I will share in this study. Although many sincere believers are mislead by popular financial teachings that encourage people to manipulate or bribe God, throughout His Word God does promise to bless us abundantly as we share what He has given us.

I could tell you of many other miracles of God's marvelous provision. No doubt you have experienced them in your life, in your home, your church. We cannot outgive God, whether it is in time commitment, finances, or the dedication of our abilities. Our unmerited reward is that we have a Father who delights in giving good gifts to His children.

Would you like to know and experience this joyful adventure of giving by faith?

Preparation is essential for any journey. If you plan to go white-water rafting on the Colorado River, for example, you would need to collect your equipment and pack food and personal items for the trip. Most importantly, you would select a guide who knows the currents, and who can handle emergencies and accidents.

Our Guide for our Christian adventure in giving is God and His Word. In the fifty years I have walked with our Lord, I have learned many things about His promises and His faithfulness. I have learned to trust God more than myself or any financial institution. I have known many of the rich and powerful of the world. I have observed individuals accumulate vast wealth and have witnessed many lose their fortunes because of financial circumstances. Those who have a biblical perspective in giving are able to handle prosperity with humility and poverty without emotional stress and discouragement.

I have prepared this Bible study to help you understand biblical principles for giving. I urge you to prayerfully and carefully follow the principles outlined in this Step. Make available to God every facet of your time, talent, and resources. I assure you on the authority of God's integrity and the promises of His holy, inerrant Word that you will enjoy a miraculous and exciting adventure in giving.

Bill Bright

What This Study Will Do for You

God has established principles for giving—of our time, talent, and resources—so that we can not only enjoy His abundance but invest strategically and generously to help fulfill the Great Commission. All that we have we receive by the grace of God, and He has put into our hands the responsibility to manage these possessions. But managing what God has given us requires an understanding of our role in His economy. We do not need to operate blindly or from ignorance. I have prepared this study to help you enter into His blessings. You will benefit from these lessons in three ways:

First, *by learning sound biblical principles for giving.* Following these principles will enable you to enjoy the promised blessings of God in your life. Ignoring these principles invites disaster. The person who disobeys God in giving cannot walk in the fullness and power of the Holy Spirit. Neither can he know the full joy of the Lord and the peace of Christ in his heart.

Second, *by understanding why it is so important to obey God in giving.* You will view His claim on all the spiritual and physical aspects of your life, and you will discover how sowing generously of your resources reaps abundant rewards.

Third, *by learning how the principle of giving applies to your time, talents, and physi-*

You will learn how to recognize your natural abilities and spiritual gifts.

cal well-being, as well as your possessions. With all the tasks of life competing for your time, you will discover how to balance your responsibilities to fulfill your temporal and spiritual duties. You will learn how to recognize your natural abilities and spiritual gifts and how you can use them for God's glory. You will see the importance of taking good care of your body.

Foundation for Faith

Step 8: The Christian and Giving is part of the *Ten Basic Steps Toward Christian Maturity*, a time-tested study series designed to provide you with a sure foundation for your faith. Hundreds of thousands have benefited from this Bible study series during the almost forty years since it was first published in its original form.

When you complete Step 8, I encourage you to continue your study with the rest of the Steps.

If you are a new Christian, the *Ten Basic Steps* will acquaint you with the major doctrines of the Christian faith. By applying the principles you will learn, you will grow spiritually and find solutions to problems you are likely to face as a new believer.

If you are a mature Christian, you will discover the tools you need to help others receive Christ and grow in their faith. Your own commitment to our Lord will be affirmed, and you will discover how to develop an effective devotional and study plan.

The series includes an individual booklet for the introductory study and one for each of the ten Steps. These study guides correlate with the expanded and updated *Handbook for Christian Maturity* and *Ten Basic Steps Leader's Guide*.

Each Step reveals a different facet of the Christian life and truth, and each contains lessons for study that can be used during your personal quiet time or in a group setting.

I encourage you to pursue the study of Step 8 with an open, eager mind. As you read, continually pray that God will show you how to relate the principles you learn to your own situation. Begin to apply them on a daily basis, and you will experience the exciting adventure of giving by faith.

How to Use This Study

On page 12 of this Step, you will find the preparatory article, "Rejoicing in His Abundance, Sharing His Resources." The article will give you a clear perspective on our purpose for living as Christians: We are not here merely to enjoy the good life; we are here as servants of God to invest our time, our talents, and our treasures to "seek and save" the lost. This is what our Lord came to do nearly 2,000 years ago, and what He commanded His followers to do generation after generation until His blessed return (Mark 16:15; Matthew 28:19). Read the article carefully before you begin Lesson 1. Review it prayerfully during your study.

This Step contains eight lessons plus a "Recap" or review. Each lesson is divided into two sections: the Bible Study and the Life Application. Begin by noting the Objective for the lesson you are studying. The Objective states the main goal for your study. Keep it in mind as you continue through the lesson.

Take time to memorize the referenced Scripture verses. Learn each verse by writing it on a small card to carry with you. You can buy cards for these verses at any bookstore or print shop, or you can make your own by using filing cards. Review daily the verses you have memorized.

Your most important objective is to meet with God in a loving, personal way.

Our Lord has commanded that we learn His Word. Proverbs 7:1–3 reminds us:

> My son, keep my words and store up my commands within you. Keep my commands and you will live; guard my teachings as the apple of your eye. Bind them on your fingers; write them on the tablet of your heart.

As you meditate on the verses you have memorized and claim God's promises, you will experience the joy, victory, and power that God's Word gives to your Christian walk. When you have finished all the studies in the entire series, you will be able to develop your own Bible study, continuing to use a systematic method for memorizing God's Word.

How to Study the Lessons

Casual Bible reading uncovers valuable spiritual facts that lie near the surface. But understanding the deeper truths requires study. Often the difference between reading and studying is a pen and notepad.

Every lesson in this study covers an important topic and gives you an opportunity to record your answers to the questions. Plan to spend a minimum of thirty minutes each day—preferably in the morning—in Bible study, meditation, and prayer.

Remember, the most important objective and benefit of a quiet time or Bible study is not to acquire knowledge or accumulate biblical information but to meet with God in a loving, personal way.

Here are some suggestions to help you in your study time:

◆ Plan a specific time and place to work on these studies. Make an appointment with God; then keep it.

◆ Have a pen or pencil, your Bible, and this booklet.

◆ Begin with prayer for God's presence, blessing, and wisdom.

◆ Meditate on the Objective to determine how it fits into your circumstances.

◆ Memorize the suggested verses.

◆ Proceed to the Bible study, trusting God to use it to teach you. Prayerfully anticipate His presence with you. Work carefully, reading the Scripture passages and thinking through the questions. Answer each as completely as possible.

◆ When you come to the Life Application, answer the questions honestly and begin to apply them to your own life.

◆ Prayerfully read through the lesson again and reevaluate your Life Application answers. Do they need changing? Or adjusting?

◆ Review the memory verses.

◆ Consider the Objective again and determine if it has been accomplished. If not, what do you need to do?

◆ Close with a prayer of thanksgiving, and ask God to help you grow spiritually in the areas He has specifically revealed to you.

◆ When you complete the first eight lessons of this Step, spend some extra time on the Recap to make sure you understand every lesson thoroughly.

◆ If you need more study of this Step, ask God for wisdom again and go through whatever lesson(s) you need to review, repeating the process until you do understand and are able to apply the truths to your own life.

These studies are not intended as a complete development of Christian beliefs. However, a careful study of the material will give you, with God's help, a sufficient understanding of how you can know and apply God's plan for your life. The spiritual truths contained here will help you meet with our Lord Jesus Christ in an intimate way and discover the full and abundant life that Jesus promised (John 10:10).

Do not rush through the lessons. Take plenty of time to think through the questions. Meditate on them. Absorb the truths presented and make the application a part of your life. Give God a chance to speak to you, and let the Holy Spirit teach you. As you spend time with our Lord in prayer and study, and as you trust and obey Him, you will experience the amazing joy of His presence (John 14:21).

Rejoicing in His Abundance, Sharing His Resources

Arthur DeMoss, one of my best friends and for many years a member of our Campus Crusade board of directors, was a gifted and godly businessman. He built one of the most successful businesses of its kind in America and in the process gained a fortune of an estimated half billion dollars.

Then suddenly, during an economic recession, stock in his company plummeted. He lost $360 million in only four months—an average of $3 million a day, more than anyone had previously lost in such a short time.

One would think that he would have been devastated and would have to cut back on his Christian giving. Instead, he *increased* it. As we talked during that period, Art was rejoicing in the Lord.

"The Lord gave me everything I have," he explained. "It all belongs to Him, and if He wants to take it away that's His business. I don't lose any sleep. I still have a wonderful family. I will do anything God wants me to do. If He takes away everything He has entrusted to me and calls me to the mission field, I'm ready to go. All He needs to do is tell me."

Art placed his trust completely in his Lord and not in his fortune. God honored his faith and obedience and eventually restored all that he had lost and much more. Art has

God is the owner of all that we possess and the total source of all our supply.

now gone to be with the Lord, but his fortune is still being used for the glory of God.

Art's story illustrates an amazingly liberating principle: If we faithfully use all that God entrusts to us, and if we keep His ownership of everything in our lives clearly in focus, any material loss simply represents His decision to direct to another the management of that possession.

This concept removes the burdensome grief associated with losing what we consider our own, since in fact it is not our own. In times of tragedy, God never forsakes us. He supplies all of our needs. Our task is to trust Him completely.

When God entrusts us with His blessings, He gives us "stewardship" over them. A young boy put it well when he responded to a question on the meaning of stewardship. "It means that life is like a ship loaded with a cargo of many things on its way to many people in many places," he said. "God is the owner, but I am the captain of the ship, and He holds me responsible for the distribution."

In the New Testament, two different words describe a *steward*. One emphasizes guardianship over children and the administration of a master's household. The other stresses the role of a manager over property. In either case, a steward oversees the affairs and property of another person.

God is the owner of all that we possess and the total source of all of our supply. He has placed us in stewardship over these treasures. This principle applies not only to our financial resources, but to all that we possess—including our time and talents—and to all that we are.

One cannot overemphasize the importance of this truth. Stewardship over all that God entrusts to us in life is foundational to giving. He has put into our hands the administration of a portion of all that He owns. As our preeminent Master, He holds us accountable for how well we manage what He has entrusted to our care (Matthew 25:14–30; Romans 14:12).

Giving by faith is meant by God to be an exciting privilege. When you honor and praise God through your commitment and obedience to stewardship, He showers you with joy. He turns your giving into a thrilling adventure in Christian living.

I have discovered and want to share with you seven principles that you can live by in order to receive God's abundant blessings through your faithful stewardship.

First, *everything you "own" actually belongs to God.* All that we have, we possess by the grace and gift of God. Everything belongs to Him. The psalmist records, "The earth is the Lord's, and everything in it, the world, and all who live in it" (Psalm 24:1). God's ownership is eternal and unchanging. He never has given up this right—and never will.

God has placed in our trust a measure of time, a unique set of talents, and sufficient resources to carry out His will for each of our lives. Our task as faithful stewards is to manage those blessings in order to bring the maximum glory to His name.

Second, *giving produces abundance.* Acts 20:35 records the words of the Lord Jesus, "It is more blessed to give than to receive." Why? Because when you give freely of yourself and of your possessions as a material expression of your spiritual obedience to Christ, God in turn meets your needs abundantly (Luke 6:38).

This is true whether you are rich or poor, whether you serve God in a land that is blessed with great material wealth or in a poverty-stricken part of the world. Most Christians have not learned to give, either out of their abundance or out of their poverty and, therefore, are not experiencing the reality of that promise.

You can never outgive God. It is a law of God that His blessings back to you always greatly exceed what you give to Him. Giving begins an endless circle of joy. God gives; you receive. You give; He receives. He then multiplies your gift back to you in the form of additional supply.

It is important to remember that God is the one who initiates this process of blessing. The purpose of the return is not just to reward you for giving, but to increase your ability to give more to further the cause of His Kingdom and help fulfill the Great Commission. Thus the circle is completed again and again (2 Corinthians 9:6–8, 10,11).

Third, *give by faith*. Simply defined, giving by faith is taking God at His Word and giving generously in anticipation of His faithful provision. Paul wrote, "My God shall supply all your need according to His riches in glory by Christ Jesus" (Philippians 4:19, NKJ).

We see from this verse that the premise of giving by faith is threefold.

1. God is the absolute source of our supply.
2. Giving is based on His resources, not our own.
3. Christ is our link to God's inexhaustible riches.

As children of God, we sit with Him in the heavenly places as joint heirs with Christ, blessed "in the heavenly realms with every spiritual blessing in Christ" (Ephesians 2:6; 1:3). The moment we received Christ as our Savior and Lord, we received this inheritance (Ephesians 1:14). Because of our Lord's glorified position in heaven, and since He is with us now through His Holy Spirit, we have all sufficiency in Him.

Fourth, *what you sow, you will reap*. On the third day of creation God commanded, "Let the earth burst forth with every sort of grass and seed-bearing plant, and fruit trees with seeds inside the fruit, so that these seeds will produce the kinds of plants and fruits they came from" (Genesis 1:11, TLB). While this passage refers to the cycles of nature, we see the principle at work in all aspects of life, spiritual as well as physical.

Using this principle to emphasize spiritual truth, Paul wrote:

> A man will always reap just the kind of crop he sows! If he sows to please his own wrong desires, he will be planting seeds of evil and he will surely reap a harvest of spiritual decay and death; but if he plants the good things of the Spirit, he will reap the everlasting life which the Holy Spirit gives him (Galatians 6:7,8, TLB).

Making it clear that the law of sowing and reaping applies to our material goods as well, Paul said:

> God, who gives seed to the farmer to plant, and later on, good crops to harvest and eat, will give you more and more seed to plant and will make it grow so that you can give away more and more fruit from your harvest (2 Corinthians 9:10, TLB).

This was written to the Corinthian Church in the context of giving financially to meet the needs of others, but it can apply to anything we give—love, joy, peace; time to care for the sick, orphans, prisoners, or a needy widow; sharing our talents to make our communities better places to live.

The law of sowing and reaping is simple: to reap anything, we must first plant a seed. To reap a bountiful harvest we must sow our best seed. This means that the best of our life—the best of our time, the best of our talents, the best of our treasure, the best of everything we have—should be on the altar of sacrifice to God.

Fifth, *give to glorify God.* As a steward of God's resources, we have but one purpose—to glorify Him. It is easy to let the day-to-day demands on our finances turn our eyes from this aim unless we clearly define our priorities. God's holy Word does this for us.

Our number one priority is God. Our second priority is our spouse. The third is our children. Other members of our family come next.

Since the family was the first institution formed by our Creator (Genesis 1:27,28), no conflict exists between the preeminence of God and the priority of family. Rather, meeting the needs of our families is a scriptural mandate and an evidence of faith (1 Timothy 5:8).

Also, it glorifies God when we help nonbelievers see the life-changing power of Jesus Christ through our caring for the poor, orphans, and widows, and through our gifts of time, talent, and treasure to agencies concerned for the welfare of the community.

But our top priority is to love, obey, and glorify God. Putting God and the fulfillment of our Lord's Great Commission first in our time, talents, and treasure must be the primary goal of our stewardship. This involves giving to the kingdom of God through our local church and mission organizations that faithfully exalt our Lord, proclaim His holy, inspired Word, and actively work toward the fulfillment of the Great Commission. It is poor stewardship to invest resources God has entrusted to us in any church or mission cause that is not directly related to discipleship, evangelism, and the fulfillment of our Lord's commands.

Sixth, *give from the heart*. Motives are an essential part of good stewardship, for they determine our reasons for giving.

Godly motives stem from a cheerful, loving heart for God. We give to please our Lord and express our love to Him. We give out of obedience to our Lord's command to lay up treasures in heaven. We give to be a channel of God's abundant resources to a desperately needy world. We give to help fulfill the Great Commission and thus help reach the world for Christ (Luke 12:43; 1 Timothy 6:5,6; 2 Corinthians 5:9; Matthew 28:19).

Maintaining right motives through the power of the Holy Spirit is essential if we are to accomplish this objective to the glory of God.

Finally, *God wants you to be financially free*. This means having enough to meet all of your financial obligations, provide adequately for your household, and give generously and joyfully to God's work.

God wants us to be financially free so we can put Him first in our life and be sensitive to His voice, ready to follow Him whenever —and wherever—He leads. If this is God's plan, why do many Christians live in financial bondage? Because they do not understand or obey biblical principles of stewardship, and they surrender to the world's philosophy of money. They burden themselves with the material concerns of life and make little or no commitment to God's work.

Many sincere Christians are in such financial bondage because of poor stewardship and planning that even when God calls them to serve Him, they are unable to obey. Such disobedience robs them of their joy, peace, victory, and fruitful witness.

Materialism isn't just a Western problem. People in all countries and cultures—from New York to Paris to Calcutta to Nairobi to remote villages along the Amazon—wrestle with some form of materialism.

Bailey Marks, vice president for International Affairs for Campus Crusade for Christ, relates a story that illustrates this:

> One day a friend of mine was visiting a pastor in a remote African village. His house was very plain. Built of sticks and mud, it had only a dirt floor and its sparse furnishings were crudely constructed.

My friend asked the pastor, "What is one of the most difficult problems you face in your ministry?"

Without hesitation, the pastor slapped his hand on the table and exclaimed, "Materialism! If my people have one pig, they want two. If they have two pigs, they want a cow, or several cows…"

When I first heard the story, I had a good laugh. But then I realized how true this is of all of us.

It is in the faithful stewardship of what God entrusts to us, not materialism, that we find fulfillment and true meaning to life.

"Financial Breathing"

True financial freedom requires spiritual health. For many years, I have taught the principle of "Spiritual Breathing." In Spiritual Breathing, we exhale the impurities of sin by confession. The Bible promises that if you confess your sins to God, He is faithful and just to forgive us and to purify us from all unrighteousness (1 John 1:9).

We inhale the purity of God's righteousness by claiming the fullness of His Spirit by faith. This is based on God's *command* in Ephesians 5:18 ("be filled with the Spirit") and His *promise* in 1 John 5:14,15 ("if we ask anything according to His will, He hears us").

Relating this principle to giving of our resources, the term "Financial Breathing" seems to apply. Following this exercise will help you preserve your financial freedom and well being.

You "exhale financially" by confessing your sin of claiming personal ownership of the resources God has entrusted to you and of withholding those resources from God's work—as though, because you earned them, by right they actually belong to you.

You "inhale financially" by acknowledging His lordship over all of your time, talents, and treasure and by sharing with others the abundance God provides.

This simple act of faith calls for a total, irrevocable commitment to the ownership of God over every area of your life.

Good stewardship requires that we live within our income and effectively manage credit. Satan aims to drive Christians into debt so he can drain them with worry or despair and keep them spiritually impotent and fruitless. For this reason, a faithful steward will never obligate himself to the place where he cannot, through control of his income, pay his debts.

As stewards of God's blessings, every Christian should consider how he can give to help win and disciple the largest possible number of people for Christ. Managing your credit and living by a budget are the first steps, but it is vitally important that you have a systematic plan for giving. Without a plan, the material concerns of life will keep you from making your commitment to God's work and rob you of His promised blessings.

Let me suggest giving a minimum of 10 percent of your income before taxes or any other deduction to the work of the Lord as a *realistic starting point*.

The practice of giving 10 percent is called "tithing," and is common among Christians today as a systematic method for giving. The word *tithe* comes from a Greek word simply meaning *the tenth* and usually refers to giving 10 percent of one's income or resources to the kingdom of God.

Early biblical records date the origin of the tithe to Abraham. He gave a tenth of his spoils of war to Melchizedek, the King of Salem and the priest of the Most High God (Genesis 14:17–20). As the spiritual father of every Christian believer (Romans 4:16), Abraham set an example for us to follow.

During the Mosaic period of the Old Testament, tithing became a requirement of the Law as a means of supporting God's work. "The purpose of tithing," Moses said, "is to teach you always to put God first in your lives" (Deuteronomy 14:23, TLB). But many argue against tithing today on the grounds that we are no longer under the Law, but now live by grace. They assert that, if under law the Israelites gave at least a tenth, under grace we should surely give more as God prospers us (1 Corinthians 16:2). On this basis, many advocate "proportional giving," but not necessarily a tenth. I agree. For most people, however, a tenth is a good starting point.

Obedience to our Lord's commands in every facet of our lives is the key to experiencing the presence of Christ and the joy of heaven. Jesus says, "The one who obeys me is the one who loves me. I will only reveal myself to those who love me and obey me. The Father will love them too, and we will come to them and live with them" (John 14:21,23, TLB).

When we obey God in our giving, we place ourselves under His protection and unlock the windows of blessing. Outside God's financial covering, however, we are vulnerable to Satan's attacks. The enemy delights in draining our resources, thereby robbing us of the ability to further God's kingdom. But our Lord promised, "I will rebuke the devourer for your sakes, so that he will not destroy the fruit of your ground" (Malachi 3:11, NKJ). Faithfulness in tithing brings great reward, for God also promised to "open the floodgates of heaven and pour out so much blessing that you will not have room enough for it" (Malachi 3:10).

Unfaithfulness or disobedience in giving not only opens the door to Satan's attacks, but displeases God and invites His discipline. One of the first questions I ask a Christian who is experiencing financial difficulty is, "Are you tithing?" If not, I cannot offer much help and encouragement until he obeys God and becomes a faithful tither.

Frequently I inquire of my wife and others who keep record of our finances, "Are we current in our tithes and offerings?" I would rather go without food than rob God of what I owe Him (Malachi 3:7–10). I love God too much to disobey Him, but I know that He will discipline me if I do disobey Him in this or any other way.

Are you experiencing the presence of Christ in your life? Do you know His joy, His love, His peace, the sense of His direction? If not, could it be that you are not obeying His commands? When you withhold the resources that God has entrusted to you for His work, He has little with which to bless you, and your life becomes unfruitful and unhappy.

I urge you to develop a personal strategy for giving that will enable you to give wisely and significantly to the kingdom of God. Acknowledge God as the source and owner of your possessions, and be ready to give an account of your stewardship to Him. Offer your gifts to the Lord Jesus as an act of praise and worship. Put God first in your giving. And manage your time, talents, and resources to bring maximum glory to His name by laying up an abundance of treasures in heaven. In so doing, you too will experience the wonderful adventure of living and giving by faith—rejoicing in His abundance and sharing His resources.

God's Ownership Over All

As Christian stewards we must realize that in Christ "we live and move and have our being" (Acts 17:28). In this lesson, you will see the basis of God's claim on your life.

Jesus Christ created us (Colossians 1:16). He bought us with His precious blood (1 Peter 1:18,19). And God anointed Him as our Lord (Ephesians 1:20–23; Acts 10:36; Romans 10:12). Thus, the whole of our life—our personality, influence, material substance, everything—is His, even our successes.

The Bible tells us that since Christ died for us, "those who live should no longer live for themselves but for him who died for them and was raised again" (2 Corinthians 5:15).

Objective: To surrender everything we have to God because we can rest in His ownership of all

Read: Genesis 1–3

Memorize: 1 Chronicles 29:11

Fall of Man	Reconciliation with God
God	God

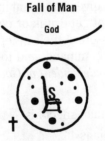
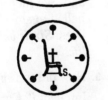

S – Self is on the throne
† – Christ is outside the life

Result: Separation from God, discord and chaos in life

† – Christ is on the throne of life

Result: Order, and stewardship evident

21

Not to acknowledge and act upon God's total ownership of every-thing we are, have, and will be is to rob ourselves of His blessing and make ourselves unfit for His service (2 Timothy 2:15,16,19–21).

Bible Study

Creation and Fall of Man

1. After what pattern did God create man (Genesis 1:26)?

in his own image

Theologians have long debated just what it is in man that constitutes the image of God. That image seems to include the basic characteristics of personality: intellect, emotion, and will. Adam and Eve had intellect (Genesis 2:19), emotion (Genesis 3:10), and will (Genesis 3:6), just as God does.

2. What did man do to bring about separation between him-self and God (Genesis 3:1–7)?

disobeyed God

Note: This passage gives important insight into the character of sin. Adam did not get drunk or commit immoral acts. He and Eve merely asserted their independence from God, re-belled against His command, and took control of their own lives. *Sin is being independent of God and running your own life.*

3. How did the sin of man affect his:

Intellect (2 Corinthians 4:2,4)?

Emotions (Jeremiah 17:9)?

Will (Romans 6:20)?

4. How did this act of rebellion affect the world
(Romans 5:12)?

Reconciliation

1. How did God bring us back and reconcile us to Himself
(Romans 5:8–10)?

2. What has God given us to enable us to live for Him
(John 14:26)?

Our Responsibility

1. God now has restored us to a position of fellowship similar
to what Adam had. What does that declare about our
present relationship with God (1 Corinthians 6:19,20)?

2. What, then, is to be our response to God (Romans 12:1,2)?

3. Many people attempt to compromise and give God less than full allegiance. How did Jesus regard that practice in Matthew 12:30?

4. In Revelation 3:15,16, how did Jesus describe His attitude toward those who will stand neither for nor against Him?

5. What logical choice did Elijah present to the people (1 Kings 18:21)?

If Elijah's logic is true, we must take one of two positions. If we determine that Jesus Christ is Lord and God, we must serve Him loyally. If He is not, He is an imposter and Christianity is obviously a hoax. If this were true, we should dissuade men from being Christians. It is one or the other! We must stand either with Christ or against Him, but never try to stand in between.

LIFE APPLICATION

1 Read Isaiah 48:17–19. What blessings would you lose by going your own way and failing to recognize God's ownership?

2 How much of your life are you willing for God to control?

How much of it does He control?

3 Is there something in your life that you have not surrendered to the control of your heavenly Father?

What is it and how will you now deal with it?

4 What do you think God will do with your life if you surrender it all to Him?

❖   ❖   ❖

Examples of Perfect Giving

Giving began with God. His supernatural expression of giving was in the sacrifice of His only begotten Son that we might receive forgiveness for our sins, become children of God, and enjoy eternal life.

God continues to give of Himself today in love, forgiveness, peace, power, and purpose. By this He enables us to live full, meaningful lives.

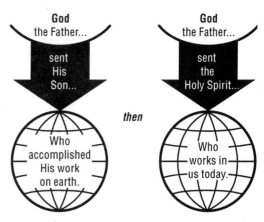

God the Father... sent His Son... Who accomplished His work on earth.

then

God the Father... sent the Holy Spirit... Who works in us today.

❖

Objective: To follow biblical examples of stewardship

Read: Luke 23–24; Colossians 1–2

Memorize: John 8:28

Giving was the lifestyle of our Lord Jesus. A concise description of His lifestyle appears in the Book of Acts, which records, "He went around doing good" (Acts 10:38). Jesus gave in feeding the multitudes. He gave in healing the sick. He gave in teaching His disciples.

He gave in empowering His disciples for evangelism. He gave in compassion for the poor. He gave in offering rest to the weary. He gave in dying on the cross for our sins. He gave in sending His Holy Spirit.

Giving is also an attribute of the Holy Spirit. He strengthens and encourages us (Acts 9:31), renews us (Titus 3:5), reveals things to us (Luke 2:26), and helps us (John 14:6, NASB). He leads and guides us (Luke 4:1; Acts 13:2,4; John 16:13), brings the love of God to us (Romans 5:5), teaches us (Luke 12:12; John 14:26), and empowers us (Acts 1:8; 4:31).

Nowhere can we find more perfect models of stewardship than in God the Father, God the Son, and God the Holy Spirit. As you study this lesson, prayerfully consider how you can apply their examples to your life.

Bible Study

Stewardship of God the Father

1. Read John 3:16. What was God's greatest gift to mankind?

2. What else does God give us (Romans 2:4,7; 1 John 5:11)?

3. Read John 3:34, 10:10, and 14:16. What has the Father given us to enable us to live abundantly?

4. List some characteristics of God's nature that make giving a priority with Him.

Stewardship of God the Son

1. List acts of Christ that indicate perfection in His stewardship (Philippians 2:5–8).

2. What was Christ's supreme purpose in life (John 6:38; Hebrews 10:7)?

3. Read John 12:23–33.

As part of God's will for Jesus, what was involved (verses 23,27,32,33)?

In verse 24, Jesus uses the example of a grain of wheat that is planted in the earth. In what sense does a grain of wheat have to "die" to bring forth fruit?

How does that apply to us (compare verse 25)?

If, as a Christian, you are unwilling to make any sacrifice to reach others for Christ, to suffer any hardship, to face any self-denial, to suffer any persecution, but instead you want everything to be comfortable, easy, and effortless, how will this affect your fruit-bearing?

4. List some characteristics of Christ's nature that make giving a priority with Him.

Stewardship of God the Holy Spirit

1. What are some duties the Holy Spirit performs as God's steward, as revealed in the following verses?

John 16:7–11

Con victing

In what way does this convicting ministry of the Holy Spirit help us in evangelism?

the Holy spirit is the one who close the convicting

John 16:13

Note: In a general way, the Holy Spirit guides the believer into spiritual truth. In a specific way, He guided the apostles and early Christians in proclaiming the truth of the gospel and in writing the New Testament Scriptures.

Romans 5:5

Gods love is poureed out

Romans 8:14

the spirit leads the sons of GOD.

Romans 8:16

His spirit testifys to ours.

Romans 8:26

2. When the Holy Spirit controls a person, who is glorifed (John 16:14)?

"He"   Jesus Christ

3. List characteristics of the Holy Spirit's nature that make giving a priority with Him.

LOVE
Presistance
Glory Christ

LIFE APPLICATION

1 How does the giving nature of God the Father inspire you to give?

Chist gave all

2 How can you best apply to your life the example that Jesus set? Be specific.

Christ live out the altment exsample

3 What does the Holy Spirit want to do in your life at this time?

4 List ways you can cooperate as suggested in Acts 4:31, Ephesians 5:18–20, and Romans 12:1,2.

❖ ❖ ❖

Stewardship of Our Time

Does the principle of tithing apply equally to our time as it does to our money?

How much of our time should we set aside for the work of the Lord each week?

How are you using the time God has given you?

Time is the heritage of every person. Whether a king or street sweeper, an astronomer or truck driver, a business tycoon or grocery clerk, each of us has the same number of hours.

Many necessities and opportunities demand much of our day. Our work takes up a large percentage of our life. Being a good husband or wife, father or mother, employer or employee requires time.

As Christians, we have spiritual priorities as well. How many hours or days in a month should we set aside for evangelism and discipleship and the ministries of our church? What about caring for the poor, the orphans, and widows as God's Word commands (James 1:27; Galatians 2:10)?

Objective: To become wise stewards of all that God has created us to be individually

Read: Romans 12

Memorize: Galatians 2:20

With all these tasks competing for our time, how can we balance our responsibilities to fulfill our temporal and spiritual duties?

As a good steward, you must manage your time wisely. Let me suggest a way to accomplish this task that Christians seldom consider today—tithing your time.

Tithing reflects a thankful, obedient attitude and acknowledges God as the source and owner of all that we possess. A voluntary act of worship, tithing teaches us to put God first. A faithful steward serves because he has such a heart for God. As we has seen, everything we have is a gift from God. Every second of every minute, every minute of every hour, twenty-four hours a day belong to Him. Although God's Word does not specifically require us to tithe our time, our Lord did command us to put Him first in all things (Matthew 6:31–33). Giving back a percentage of our time enables us to give God priority and assures that we will fulfill our service to Him.

❖

Bible Study

Right Attitude About Time
Read Psalm 90:12.

1. What should be our prayer concerning the use of the time that God gives us?

   use our time wisely -
   we need wisdom in making choices

2. Why is the proper use of our time today so important (James 4:13–15)?

   we do not know what a day brings

3. What does God demand of us in the stewardship of our time (Psalm 62:8)?

   trust in Him - Pour out your heart

When do you find this hardest to do?

tired, when things are going well

4. What does Christ admonish us to do as stewards of time until He comes again (Mark 13:33–37)?

Be ready — be alert —

5. If we are wise stewards and heed the commands of our Lord, how will we use our time (Ephesians 5:15,16)?

make most of every opportunity

What does making use of our time have to do with wisdom?

With evil days?

Right Relationship With God

1. As wise stewards concerned over the use of our time, what will we want to understand (Ephesians 5:17)?

The Lords will

2. What is necessary in order to know fully the will of God concerning the duties of our stewardship (Ephesians 5:18)?

Be filled w/ the Spirit

3. What will the Holy Spirit give the faithful steward to enable him to perform the duties of stewardship (Acts 1:8)?

power

4. In whose name should the steward perform these duties (Colossians 3:17)?

Jesus Christ

5. What should be our attitude as we utilize the time over which God has made us stewards (Ephesians 5:19–21)?

grateful

6. How would you describe such a useful and joyous life (John 10:10)?

full & abundant

Most Important Use of Time

1. As wise stewards who know and are obedient to the will of God, what will we spend much of our time aggressively doing (Mark 16:15)?

preaching the gospel

2. What does God say about a soul winner in Proverbs 11:30?

wise

3. Of what value is a soul according to Christ in Mark 8:36,37?

4. What is the greatest thing that has happened in your life?

5. What, then, is the greatest thing you can do for another?

6. What happens in God's presence when one repents and receives Christ (Luke 15:7,10)?

7. How did Paul feel about those whom he had won to Christ (1 Thessalonians 2:19,20)?

LIFE APPLICATION

Keeping track of how you spend your day can be of great value in evaluating the stewardship of your time. On a sheet of paper, record the number of hours spent on business, class, sleep, Christian service, recreation, etc. Place the total hours per week used in each activity on the chart below.

STEWARDSHIP OF TIME	
Study and class _____	Activities and athletics _____
Devotional life _____	Commuting _____
Christian service _____	Employment_____
Rest _____	Laundry and clean-up _____
Recreation and social life _____	Miscellaneous _____

1 Determine what blocks of time are wasteful. How could you use them to serve the Lord?

2 List ways to tithe your time that can be worked into your present schedule.

Stewardship of Our Bodies

Some time ago, my heart grieved as I learned of a respected Christian leader who had fallen into a life of sin. He had obviously not intended to do so, but when the temptation came, he yielded. As a result, his wife, his family, his friends, and fellow Christians suffered heartache. Most tragically, his testimony and witness for the Lord Jesus has suffered untold damage. Many have ridiculed and rejected the cause of Christ because of his sin.

Since God wants us to live a holy life, the enemy seeks to entrap us in sin and defeat. One of Satan's methods is to tempt us to misuse our bodies.

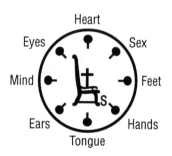

Objective: To surrender our bodies to Christ, from the heart

Read: Psalm 51; Galatians 5; Ephesians 5

Memorize: Psalm 139:23,24

But God created our bodies for His glory. By surrendering them to Him, He can use us to further His kingdom and help us grow in our faith.

This study will help you understand the importance of giving control of your body to God. You will also discover danger areas in using your physical self and how to help further the cause of Christ with different parts of your body.

Bible Study

The Spirit and the Body

Read 1 Peter 4:1,2 and Hebrews 10:1–10.

1. How did Jesus regard His body (1 Peter 4:1,2)?

*not as his own
But for Christ*

2. What does Christ's sacrifice mean to us (Hebrews 10:10)?

*Because of what he did
we are made holy*

Look up the word *sanctified* in a Bible dictionary. How does the word relate to your stewardship?

3. What do you learn about the body of the Christian from Romans 8:8,9 and Romans 12:1?

4. Express in your own words the additional reasons given in 1 Corinthians 6:19,20 for being a good steward of your body.

How are we to do this (Galatians 5:16; Romans 12:1; Matthew 26:41)?

Individual Parts of the Body

1. The tongue

Why is it so important to be a good steward of the tongue (James 3:2–6; James 1:26)?

What should you know concerning its use (Matthew 12:36)?

List areas in which you misuse your tongue.

How has this affected your life?

How should you use your tongue properly (James 3:9,10; Ephesians 4:29; Proverbs 21:23; Psalm 39:1; Proverbs 4:24)?

2. The heart

What must we understand about the heart (Jeremiah 17:9)?

How can we counteract our natural tendencies (Psalm 139:23,24)?

What condition of heart does God require (Psalm 51:17)?

What kind of heart does God look for and why (2 Chronicles 16:9; Matthew 5:8; 2 Thessalonians 3:5; Psalm 15:1,2)?

3. The mind

What is your responsibility in being a steward of your mind (1 Peter 1:13)?

Whose mind should you have and which qualities should you strive for (Philippians 2:5–8; 1 Corinthians 2:12–16)?

What is the result of keeping your mind focused on God (Isaiah 26:3)?

How can you keep your mind on Him (Philippians 4:6,7; Deuteronomy 11:18)?

4. The hands

What does God think about the work of your hands (Proverbs 12:14,24)?

How did the apostles feel about the importance of what
their hands had done (Acts 20:34,35; 1 Thessalonians 4:11,12)?

How can we use our hands to glorify God?
Proverbs 31:20

Ephesians 5:28

Deuteronomy 15:10,11

Ecclesiastes 9:10

5. The feet
Contrast the feet of those who do evil with those who do
good (Isaiah 59:7; Romans 3:15; Isaiah 52:7; Psalm
119:101,105; 56:13).

How do Romans 10:15 and Ephesians 6:15 relate to
evangelism?

6. The eyes
What is the importance of the eyes (Matthew 6:22,23)?

Describe what this means to you.

What sins can we commit with our eyes?
Proverbs 21:4

Jeremiah 22:17

Proverbs 27:20

Matthew 5:28

1 John 2:16

What privilege did the apostles have (1 John 1:1–3)?

How can we avoid temptation (Psalm 19:8; 119:37; 121:1,2; 123:1)?

7. The ears
Write down ways we can misuse hearing.
Proverbs 21:13

2 Timothy 4:3,4

What can listening to God give us?
Romans 10:17

John 5:24

How can you apply James 1:19,22 to your daily life? Give specific examples.

Sexual Expression

1. Compare the sexual sins in 1 Corinthians 6:9,10,13–18 with marriage in 1 Corinthians 7:1–8.

2. God considered David a man after His own heart, yet what was David's great sin (2 Samuel 11:2–5,14–17,26,27)?

3. What is God's stern judgment against misusers and abusers of sex (1 Corinthians 6:9,10)?

Why is it especially tragic if a Christian becomes involved in the misuse of sex (1 Corinthians 6:15–18)?

How serious is sexual lust, according to Christ (Matthew 5:28)?

4. How can the application of the following verses enable you to overcome sexual lust?

Philippians 4:8

Psalm 119:11

1 Corinthians 10:13

Romans 6:11–13

1 Thessalonians 4:3–5

Psalm 119:9

List things in your life that tempt you to have impure thoughts. How can you apply these verses to each?

LIFE APPLICATION

1 How does stewardship of each individual part of the body affect each part?

How could it affect the body as a whole?

2 How would you apply 1 Thessalonians 5:22 to the following:

The use of your tongue?

The desires of your heart?

The control of your mind?

The work of your hands?

Where you go?

What you see?

What you hear?

Your conduct with members of the opposite sex?

Stewardship of Our Talents and Gifts

God created us with a great variety of talents. You may be able to run a marathon, organize a group meeting, teach, or write. Your skill may be typing, photography, or painting. Perhaps you sing or play a musical instrument. Maybe you are a carpenter, landscaper, engineer, mechanic, or bookkeeper. Each of us has a unique function to perform in life and in the Body of Christ.

Ministering
Teaching
Giving
Helping
Exhorting
Having Faith
Showing Mercy
Ruling

❖

Objective: To recognize our talents and abilities and to surrender them to God for His use and glory

Read: 1 Corinthians 12

Memorize: 1 Peter 4:10

The Bible refers to the church as the Body of Christ with Christ as its Head (1 Corinthians 12:27; Ephesians 5:23). Just as your body has many specialized parts, each with its own function, so the church is composed of many individuals, each with his own special function to perform—and contribution to make—to the rest of the Body. I encourage you to identify your talents, and ask God to show you how to use them for His glory.

Every Christian possesses both natural talents and spiritual gifts. Our natural abilities come to us at physical birth and are developed through life. Our spiritual gifts are imparted by the Holy Spirit, enabling us to minister to others in behalf of Christ.

Bible Study

Natural Gifts

1. What talents and natural abilities do you have?

2. How did you acquire them or improve on them?

3. According to 1 Corinthians 4:6,7 and Exodus 4:11, what should your attitude be about them?

4. How would you apply Colossians 3:17 to the stewardship of your natural gifts?

Spiritual Gifts

1. Major passages on spiritual gifts in the Bible are:
- ◆ Romans 12:3–8
- ◆ 1 Corinthians 12:1–31
- ◆ Ephesians 4:4–8,11–16
- ◆ 1 Peter 4:10,11

From these passages make a composite list of spiritual gifts (combine any two that might be identical). Across from each one, give your brief definition of the gift. (You may wish to consult a concordance or a Bible dictionary.)

SPIRITUAL GIFT	DEFINITION

2. What are some reasons God has given gifted people to the church (Ephesians 4:11–16)?

3. Why will two people not exercise the same gift in the same manner (1 Corinthians 12:4–6)?

4. Though some spiritual gifts seem to be of greater value than others (1 Corinthians 12:28–31), what ideas does Paul stress to keep Christians from personal pride because of those they may possess (Romans 12:4,5; 1 Corinthians 12:12–26; 1 Corinthians 13; Ephesians 4:11–16)?

5. List several principles that describe what your attitude and responsibilities should be toward your spiritual gifts (Romans 12:3–8).

LIFE APPLICATION

Follow these steps to more fully understand your part in the Body of Christ:

1 Realize that you have at least one spiritual gift, probably more (1 Corinthians 12:11).

2 Pray that God will make your gifts known to you.

3 Determine which of your activities the Lord seems to bless and inquire of other mature Christians who know you well what your spiritual gifts might be.

4 List here what you believe your spiritual gifts are.

5 Seek to develop your gifts in the power of the Holy Spirit.

6 Realize that you may have other gifts of which you are not presently aware, so exercise various gifts. Be aware that you are accountable to God for stewardship of your spiritual gifts.

❖ ❖ ❖

Stewardship of Our Possessions

One afternoon, Grandpa Clark strode into his house, pockets bulging with treats for his grandchildren. As he settled into his creaking rocker, the children clamored around him with expectant faces, each pushing and shoving to be the first to see what Grandpa had brought them.

The gray-haired man dug deep into his pockets and pulled out a fistful of candy, handing each child a favorite treat. When he finished, he leaned back in his rocker with a smile of contentment to watch them tear at the wrappings.

On his left, two jealous brothers argued over whose flavor of Lifesavers tasted better. Another child sat at his feet munching a candy bar. Suddenly, a tiny red-haired sweetheart patted her grandpa on the arm. Concern furrowed her brow.

❖

Objective: To surrender all our of material wealth to God, and to give with joy and gratitude

Read: 2 Corinthians 9; Matthew 6:19–34; 25:14–30; Luke 12:15–21

Memorize: Luke 16:13

"Would you like some of my M&Ms, Grandpa?" she asked with sad, shy eyes. "You don't have anything."

Grandpa Clark peered down at his only granddaughter and grinned. Gently, he gathered her dainty form into his lap. "Why, you haven't even opened your candy," he observed.

She stared into his eyes with a frank expression. " 'Cause I want you to have the first one."

"Why, thank you, I think I will," he smiled, carefully opening her little package. With relish, he removed a couple of colored candies and popped them into his mouth. Then he wrapped his arms tightly around her, engulfing her happy face.

This story clearly illustrates tithing—giving back to God the first part of what He has given us.

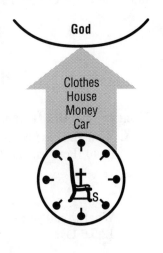

As you recall, the word *tithe* comes from a Greek term simply meaning *the tenth*. Godly principles underlay this practice. Tithing accomplishes the following:

◆ Acknowledges God as the source and owner of all that we possess

◆ Is a voluntary act of worship

◆ Teaches us to put God first

◆ Is a practical guideline for systematic giving

◆ Provides spiritual release and blessing

Tithing performs a role entirely different from that of mere giving, which suggests that we own all that we possess. Through tithing we acknowledge that God created our increase. As stewards of what God entrusted to us, we set aside a proportion to use for the cause of Christ. We never consider any part of our possessions to be our exclusive property but prayerfully tithe on the entire amount.

"The purpose of tithing," we have learned, "is to teach you always to put God first in your lives" (Deuteronomy 14:23, TLB). God does not honor a gift that comes from leftovers. He requires the first and the best of our increase (Exodus 22:29,30; Proverbs 3:9,10). Tithing ensures this.

Ten percent, an Old Testament measure for giving, is a good beginning point for a faithful and dedicated steward. And though we are not under the Law but under grace, as Dr. J. B. Gabrell declared,

"It is unthinkable from the standpoint of the cross that anyone would give less under grace than the Jews gave under law."

Measuring their giving by the grace of the cross and not by the legalism of the Law, the early Christians did not limit themselves to the tithe. They gave much more. And they gave in the Spirit of Christ, as a demonstration of His pre-eminence in their lives, to help fulfill the Great Commission.

Bible Study

Money—The Old Testament Standard

1. What did God command those under the Law of Moses to do (Leviticus 27:30; Malachi 3:8–10)?

2. What would you say the "storehouse" is (Deuteronomy 12:5,6,11)?

3. How much is a tithe (Genesis 14:20; Hebrews 7:2)?

Money—The New Testament Standard

1. As believers in Christ, we are under grace, rather than the Old Testament Law. Whereas the Law in itself did not provide eternal life for those who attempted to keep it (Galatians 2:16), we have received life by the favor of God though we do not deserve it and could not possibly earn it.

   Therefore, do we have a higher or lower motivation and standard for stewardship of our possessions than those under the Law?

2. How did Jesus regard a person's responsibility in that area (Matthew 23:23)?

3. Read 2 Corinthians 8–9.

In this passage, Paul attempts to encourage the Corinthian church to give financially to help needy Christians. He first points them to the example of the Macedonian church.

What was the attitude of the Macedonians in giving their money to God (2 Corinthians 8:2–5)?

In light of this, what do you think God is interested in?

Nevertheless, why is giving money an important part of our Christian life (2 Corinthians 8:7; 9:12,13)?

In what sense does the one who "sows" (gives) sparingly reap sparingly (2 Corinthians 9:6)?

What kind of attitude does God want you to have in giving (2 Corinthians 9:7)?

When is it hard for you to give that way?

God's Priority for Missions

1. Who is the great example of giving (2 Corinthians 8:9)?

2. In your own words, summarize the last command Jesus gave His disciples (Matthew 28:19,20).

3. Read John 14:21,23,24. Describe how this relates to fulfilling the Great Commission.

4. Oswald Smith said, "If you see ten men carrying a heavy log, nine of them on one end and one man struggling to carry the other, which end would most need your help? The end with only one man." This illustrates how inequitably the evangelized nations have been using their resources to help fulfill the Great Commission.

What percentage of your giving is going to overseas missions?

To home missions?

5. Prayerfully consider what kind of adjustments you feel the Lord is leading you to make in your missions giving. Record your decisions here.

Other Possessions

1. To whom do you and your possessions belong (Psalm 50:12; 1 Corinthians 6:19,20)?

2. What should be your motive in the use of whatever you possess (1 Corinthians 10:31)?

LIFE APPLICATION

1 What is your understanding about tithing? Describe your view in a short paragraph.

2 What is the difference between "giving" and "tithing"?

Which one describes your practice and why?

3 Ask yourself, "Is my heart attitude one of joy and gratefulness as I give?" How do you express your attitude?

4 List some Christian groups or churches that are working to fulfill the Great Commission in which you would like to invest financially.

Trusting God for Our Finances

Objective: To learn how to trust God for our finances and ask Him to supply our needs

Read: Proverbs 3:5,6; John 10:10; Matthew 6:33,34

Memorize: Psalm 12:6

Changing economic conditions exemplify the instability of finances throughout the world. Instead of placing their trust in the Lord who promised to meet all of their needs, most Christians trust in their investments, savings, and retirement plans to ensure security and happiness—only to find their hopes dashed when financial reverses deplete their assets. Many are wasting their lives trying to achieve financial security in a volatile world.

Our heavenly Father, on the other hand, wants us to enjoy a full, abundant life free from the cares and stresses brought by confidence in money and other material possessions. Rather than trusting in a worldly system that cannot assure our welfare or relying on our own weak capabilities to provide for our needs, He calls us to depend entirely on Him.

Permit me to suggest a plan that will help you release your faith in God and develop your trust in Him for your finances.

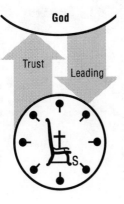

Bible Study

Recognize That God is Worthy of Your Trust

1. Read Psalm 12:6. How much can we trust God?

refined seven times

2. What will happen if you make God's promises the foundation of your financial security (Proverbs 3:5,6)?

GOD will guide us

3. List the financial areas that are hardest for you to put into God's hands. Prayerfully dedicate them to Him.

Realize That God Wants You to Live a Full and Abundant Life

1. Read John 10:10. How does this promise apply to financial freedom?

2. Does abundant life mean having all the money or possessions you want? Why or why not?

3. Do you feel you have abundant life right now? If not, what is keeping you from it?

Substitute Faith for Fear

1. How does fear interfere with your trust in God?

2. Read 2 Timothy 1:7. Contrast the two kinds of spirits mentioned.

3. Write down the financial areas that make you fearful. Surrender these to the Lord.

Ask God to Supply Your Needs

1. What is the difference between needs and wants? Be specific.

2. Why do we lack good things (James 4:2,3; John 15:7)?

3. Faith requires action. According to 1 John 5:14,15:

   a) As an act of your will, ask God to supply your needs.

   b) Expect Him, as an expression of your faith, to provide
      for your needs.

Keep Your Heart and Motives Pure

1. What wrong motives do we sometimes display (James 4:3)?

What is the result?

2. Write down the wrongful motives that you battle.

Then:

a) Confess them to God.

b) Claim the power of the Holy Spirit to help you rely on
   Him to supply your needs.

Take a Step of Faith

1. What is essential to your Christian walk (Hebrews 11:6)?

2. One way to enlarge your faith is to make a "faith promise"—
one that is greater than you are capable of fulfilling according
to your present income. It is not a pledge that must be paid.
Rather, it is a voluntary "promise" based on your faith in God's
ability to supply out of His resources what you cannot give out
of your own. You give as God supplies.

Describe a time in which God led you to give above
your means.

What was the result?

If you have never made a "faith promise," you may want to
do so now after prayerfully considering various worthwhile
investments you can make for God. Keep a careful record
of your giving and how God supplied your needs in a
special way.

LIFE APPLICATION

1 Read Luke 6:38. How does this verse apply to financial freedom?

2 Suppose a new Christian confides in you that he is afraid to give God control over his checkbook. How would you advise him?

3 Review the steps to trusting God for your finances. Which of these steps are weak areas in your life?

Why do you find them difficult?

What could you do to strengthen them?

4 Read the steps to "Financial Breathing" listed on page 18. Breathe financially for any areas in which you do not follow good stewardship principles.

5 Prayerfully consider the faith promise God would have you make. Write that promise here.

Our Accountability to God

M any Christians miss the special blessing of God because they do not obey our Lord's command recorded in the Gospel of Matthew:

> Don't store up treasures here on earth where they can erode away or may be stolen. Store them in heaven where they will never lose their value, and are safe from thieves. If your profits are in heaven your heart will be there too (Matthew 6:19–21, TLB).

Jesus knew that by storing up treasures on earth, we would soon take on the appearance of the world. Through selfish desires, we would cease to reflect the character of God and seek our own glory. By laying up treasures in heaven, on the other hand, we would declare the glory of His kingdom.

Everything we do to bring men and women into the kingdom of God, every act of kindness, every expression of love is laying up treasure in God's storehouse. We give out of love for God and gratitude for His love and sacrifice for us through the gift of His only begotten Son, our Savior Jesus Christ.

God will hold us accountable for our motivation in giving and for our faithful obed-

❖

Objective: To recognize our ultimate accountability to God

Read: Luke 19:12–27; Matthew 24 and 25

Memorize: 2 Corinthians 5:10

65

ience to our Lord's command to help fulfill the Great Commission
and so reach the world for Christ. The apostle Paul wrote:

> We will all stand before God's judgment seat. So then,
> each of us will give an account of himself to God (Romans
> 14:10,12).

Relating the parable of the shrewd manager, Jesus said:

> There was a rich man whose manager was accused of
> wasting his possessions. So he called him in and asked
> him, "What is this I hear about you? Give an account of
> your management..." (Luke 16:1,2).

God considers "an immortal soul beyond all price. There is no
trouble too great, no humiliation too deep, no suffering too severe,
no love too strong, no labor too hard, no expense too large, but that
it is worth it, if it is spent in the effort to win a soul."[1]

As faithful stewards, our primary financial responsibility is to
help worthy ministries reach the largest possible number of people
for Christ. We are accountable to our Lord's last command before
He ascended into heaven to "Go and make disciples of all nations"
(Matthew 28:19).

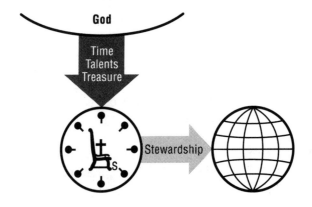

---

[1] "Junk That Missionary Barrel," *Moody Monthly* (September 1977), p.56.

Bible Study

The Christian at Christ's Coming

1. According to 2 Corinthians 5:10, what will Christ do when He comes again?

2. Notice that Paul says "we all." Who is this primarily for?

Note: Our sins have already been judged in Christ (Romans 8:1). The judgment here is of our works since the time we became a believer.

3. Read 1 Corinthians 3:11–15.

God's judgment of our works is compared to the reaction of certain materials to fire. According to this passage, what is God most interested in regarding the works we do for Him (verse 13)?

How is it then possible for us to spend long hours working for God, but have no reward whatsoever?

A Christian's works may be rejected, but what can he himself still be sure of (verse 15)?

The Time of Christ's Coming

1. The judgment of the Christian will take place when Christ comes again. When will that be (Acts 1:6,7)?

2. On what should we concentrate until He comes (Acts 1:8; Matthew 28:19,20; Mark 16:15)?

3. Why has Christ waited so long already before coming (2 Peter 3:9)?

The Earth at Christ's Coming

Read Mark 13. This chapter foretells the world conditions as Christ's coming approaches. As we see the world today becoming more like this, we know His coming is drawing nearer.

1. What will we see happening in religion (verses 5,6,21,22)?

2. What will the world situation be (verses 7,8)?

3. What will occur in nature (verse 8)?

4. What will the attitude be toward true believers (verses 12,13)?

5. Describe in your own words what you think Christ's coming will be like (verses 26,27).

Preparing for Christ's Coming

1. As a believer, what are you to do as His coming draws near (Mark 13:33)?

2. How will obedience to that instruction affect the following:
Your employment?

Your social life?

Your worship?

Your giving?

LIFE APPLICATION

1. As faithful stewards of God's resources, our primary responsibility is to help fulfill the Great Commission. If God were to call you into account for your stewardship, what would you say to Him (Luke 16:1,2; Hebrews 4:13; 1 Peter 4:5)?

   How can you be more faithful in your giving to help reach your world for Christ?

2. In what ways are you storing up treasures in heaven?

3. Look over your spending for the past month. What percentage did you give to God's work?

4. To plan your giving for the next year, go through the chart on the following page some time this week.

Stewardship Plan

1. Begin by asking God how much and where He wants you to invest your time, talents, possessions, and money. Write these ideas here.

2. Prayerfully develop a systematic plan for giving each month in each of these areas:
   ◆ Time
   ◆ Talents
   ◆ Possessions
   ◆ Money

3. Plan to set aside some time and resources for needs you may become aware of at your church, in your neighborhood, or other places.

4. Dedicate your plan to God. Ask Him to use your resources to bring the greatest glory to His name.

5. Begin to implement your plan with a joyful heart, expecting God to bless you through your stewardship.

Recap

The following questions will help you review this Step. If necessary, reread the appropriate lesson(s).

1. Define "Christian steward" in your own words.

2. Why are we referred to as Christian stewards?

3. Summarize your responsibilities as a steward of God as you now understand them.

Reread: Romans 12; 1 Corinthians 12; James 3:1,2

Review: Verses memorized

LIFE APPLICATION

1 List several things over which you exercise stewardship.

2 What is the most important thing for you to realize about your attitude toward stewardship?

3 In which particular areas of your life have you seen a change for the better in your Christian stewardship?

4 Read about the *Sound Mind Principle* on the following pages. Use the steps included to help you make financial decisions.

Maximize Your Giving Through the Sound Mind Principle

Now that you have started on your thrilling adventure of giving by faith and have begun developing a personal strategy for investing in God's kingdom, you will discover many seemingly effective avenues in which to give of your time, talents, and resources. Suddenly, you may find yourself confused about how to wisely use the resources God has entrusted to you among so many exciting choices. How does a sincere steward discover God's will for the investment of his time, talents, and resources? By applying the *Sound Mind Principle* of Scripture. Let me explain.

In 2 Timothy 1:7 the apostle Paul writes, "God has not given us a spirit of fear, but of power and of love and of a sound mind" (NKJ). The "sound mind" referred to in this verse means a well-balanced mind that is under the control of the Holy Spirit, "renewed" according to Romans 12:2:

> Do not conform any longer to the pattern of this world, but be transformed by the renewing of your mind. Then you will be able to test and approve what God's will is—His good, pleasing and perfect will.

You can know God's will for giving your time, talents, and resources.

Making a Sound Decision

Let me ask you: Do you make your decisions according to the *Sound Mind Principle?*

If you would like to know the will of God for your life according to this principle, consider these questions:

◆ *Why did Jesus come?*
He came "to seek and to save what was lost" (Luke 19:10).

◆ *What is the greatest experience of your life?*
If you are a Christian, your answer quite obviously will be, "Knowing Jesus Christ personally as my Savior and Lord."

◆ *What is the greatest thing that you can do to help others?*
The answer again is obvious, "Introduce them to Christ."

Thus, every sincere Christian will want to make his God-given time, talents, and resources available to Christ so that his fullest potential will be realized for Him. For one Christian, the talent God has given him may be prophetic preaching, evangelism, or teaching; for another, it may be business; for another, the ministry or missions; for another, homemaking.

As you evaluate the talents that God has given you, take a sheet of paper and make a list of the most logical ways through which your life can be used to accomplish the most for the glory of God. List the pros and cons of each opportunity. Where or how, according to the *Sound Mind Principle*, can the Lord Jesus Christ accomplish the most in continuing His ministry of seeking and saving the lost through you? Such a procedure will inevitably result in positive actions leading to God's perfect will for your life. But note a word of caution. The *Sound Mind Principle* is not valid unless certain conditions exist:

1. There must be no unconfessed sin in your life.

2. Your life must be fully dedicated to Christ, and you must be filled with the Holy Spirit in obedience to the command of Ephesians 5:18.

3. You must walk in the Spirit (abide in Christ) moment by moment, placing your faith in the trustworthiness of God with the confidence that the Lord is directing and will continue to direct your life according to promises in Scripture.

The counsel of others should be prayerfully considered, especially that of mature, dedicated Christians who know the Word of God and are able to relate the proper use of Scripture to your need. However, be careful not to make the counsel of others a crutch. Although God often speaks to us through other Christians, we are admonished to place our trust in Him (Proverbs 3:5,6).

Four Basic Factors

A discussion of God's will should consider four basic factors similar to the *Sound Mind Principle*. God's will is revealed in:

1. The authority of Scripture
2. Providential circumstances
3. Conviction based upon reason
4. Impressions of the Holy Spirit upon our minds according to Philippians 2:13

However, an appraisal of impressions from the Holy Spirit is safer with a mature believer than with a new or worldly (carnal) Christian because there is always the danger of misunderstanding the impressions.

Know the source of leading before responding to it. To the inexperienced, what appears to be the leading of God may not be from Him at all, but from "the rulers of darkness of this world." Satan and his helpers often disguise themselves as "angels of light" by counterfeiting the works of God to deceive His followers.

One further word of caution must be given. It is true that God still reveals His will to some men and women in dramatic ways, but this should be considered the exception rather than the rule.

God still leads today as He has through the centuries. Philip the deacon, for example, was holding a successful campaign in Samaria. The *Sound Mind Principle* would have directed him to continue his campaign. However, God overruled by a special revelation, and Philip was led by the Spirit to introduce the Ethiopian eunuch to Christ. According to tradition, God used the Ethiopian eunuch to communicate the message of our living Lord to his own country.

How You Will Know

Living according to the *Sound Mind Principle* permits such dramatic leadings of God, but we are not to wait for revelations before we start moving for Christ. Faith must have an object. A Christian's faith is built on the authority of God's Word supported by historical fact and not on any shallow emotional experience. However, a Christian's trust in God's will revealed in His Word will result in the decisions that are made by following the *Sound Mind Principle*. Usually, the confirmation that you are in God's will is a quiet, peaceful assurance that you are doing what He wants you to do with the expectancy that He will use you to bear much fruit.

The result of a life that is lived according to the *Sound Mind Principle* is the most peaceful, abundant, and fruitful life of all.

Expect the Lord Jesus Christ to draw men to Himself through you. As you begin each day, acknowledge the fact that you belong to Him. Thank Him that He lives within you. Invite Him to use your mind to think His thoughts, your heart to express His love, your lips to speak His truth. Ask Jesus to be at home in your life and to walk around in your body so that He may continue seeking and saving souls through you.

It is my sincere prayer that you may know the reality of this kind of life, that you may fully appropriate all that God has given you as your rightful heritage in Christ.

Note: This is adapted from my "Paul Brown" letter. For more information on the *Sound Mind Principle*, write to NewLife Publications, 100 Sunport Lane, Orlando, FL 32809.

Resources to Help You Be a Faithful Steward

Transferable Concept: How You Can Experience the Adventure of Giving by Bill Bright. Published by NewLife Publications, Orlando, FL.

Personal Finances by Larry Burkett. Published by Moody Press, Chicago, IL.

Financial Freedom by Larry Burkett. Published by Moody Press, Chicago, IL.

Your Financial Future by Larry Burkett. Published by Moody Press, Chicago, IL.

A Woman's Guide to Financial Peace of Mind by Ron and Judy Blue. Published by Focus on the Family Publishing, Colorado Springs, CO.

Master Your Money by Ron Blue. Published by Thomas Nelson Publishers, Nashville, TN.

Debt-Free Living by Larry Burkett. Published by Moody Press, Chicago, IL.

Available through your local Christian bookstore, mail-order catalog distributor, or NewLife Publications.

Ten Basic Steps Toward Christian Maturity

Eleven easy-to-use individual guides to help you understand the basics of the Christian faith

INTRODUCTION:
The Uniqueness of Jesus

Explains who Jesus Christ is. Reveals the secret of His power to turn you into a victorious, fruitful Christian.

STEP 1: The Christian Adventure

Shows you how to enjoy a full, abundant, purposeful, and fruitful life in Christ.

STEP 2: The Christian and the Abundant Life

Explores the Christian way of life—what it is and how it works practically.

STEP 3: The Christian and the Holy Spirit

Teaches who the Holy Spirit is, how to be filled with the Spirit, and how to make the Spirit-filled life a moment-by-moment reality in your life.

STEP 4: The Christian and Prayer

Reveals the true purpose of prayer and shows how the Father, Son, and Holy Spirit work together to answer your prayers.

STEP 5: The Christian and the Bible

Talks about the Bible—how we got it, its authority, and its power to help the believer. Offers methods for studying the Bible more effectively.

STEP 6: The Christian and Obedience

Learn why it is so important to obey God and how to live daily in His grace. Discover the secret to personal purity and power as a Christian and why you need not fear what others think of you.

STEP 7: The Christian and Witnessing

Shows you how to witness effectively. Includes a reproduction of the *Four Spiritual Laws* and explains how to share them.

STEP 8: The Christian and Giving

Discover God's plan for your financial life, how to stop worrying about money, and how to trust God for your finances.

STEP 9: Exploring the Old Testament

Features a brief survey of the Old Testament. Shows what God did to prepare the way for Jesus Christ and the redemption of all who receive Him as Savior and Lord.

STEP 10: Exploring the New Testament

Surveys each of the New Testament books. Shows the essence of the gospel and highlights the exciting beginning of the Christian church.

Leader's Guide

The ultimate resource for even the most inexperienced, timid, and fearful person asked to lead a group study in the basics of the Christian life. Contains questions and answers from the *Ten Basic Steps* Study Guides.

A Handbook for Christian Maturity

Combines the eleven-booklet series into one practical, easy-to-follow volume. Excellent for personal or group study.

Available through your local Christian bookstore, mail-order catalog distributor, or NewLife Publications.

About the Author

BILL BRIGHT is founder and president of Campus Crusade for Christ International. Serving in 152 major countries representing 98 percent of the world's population, he and his dedicated associates of nearly 50,000 full-time staff, associate staff, and trained volunteers have introduced tens of millions of people to Jesus Christ, discipling millions to live Spirit-filled, fruitful lives of purpose and power for the glory of God.

Dr. Bright did graduate study at Princeton and Fuller Theological seminaries from 1946 to 1951. The recipient of many national and international awards, including five honorary doctorates, he is the author of numerous books and publications committed to helping fulfill the Great Commission. His special focus is New Life 2000, an international effort to help reach more than six billion people with the gospel of our Lord Jesus Christ and help fulfill the Great Commission by the year 2000.